THE FESTIVAL STORYBOOK

JUHI SINHA

SCHOLASTIC
New York Toronto London Auckland
Sydney New Delhi Hong Kong

These stories were first published as individual editions by Scholastic India in 2002.

Published by Scholastic India Pvt. Ltd.
A subsidiary of Scholastic Inc., New York, 10012 (USA).
Publishers since 1920, with international operations in Canada,
Australia, New Zealand, the United Kingdom, India, and Hong Kong.

For information regarding permission, write to:
Scholastic India Pvt. Ltd.
A-27, Ground Floor, Sigma Centre
Infocity-1, Sector 34, Gurgaon 122001 (India)

First edition : August 2016
This reprint edition : December 2025

ISBN-13: 978-93-8610-641-4

Printed in India at Saurabh Printers Pvt.Ltd.

Contents

Juhi Sinha is a film maker and author. Over the last 25 years her serials and documentaries have been shown on national and international channels. Her articles, short stories and features have also been published in leading newspapers and magazines in India. Her books written for adults include *Beyond the Dunes–Journeys in Rajasthan, When Peacocks Dance–Writings on the Monsoon* and *Bismillah Khan the Maestro of Benaras*. Juhi Sinha has also authored several children's books for CBT (Children's Book Trust) and Scholastic India.

Raghu's Diwali

Illustrated by Neeta Gangopadhyay

Raghu woke up early in the morning. He was excited because Diwali was only three days away. Raghu loved Diwali, that beautiful festival when everyone lighted diyas.

Raghu's father was a potter, and Diwali was a very special festival for him and the family. He made small, earthen diyas on the potter's wheel in a corner of the courtyard.

Father was ready to take the diyas to the nearby market. But this year, he also gave Raghu a small basket full of diyas. "These are for you to sell, Raghu. You can take them to the market on your own."

Raghu took the diyas and went to the market. All day he waited for people to buy the diyas, but not a single diya was sold. Everybody bought them from another man, who was selling pretty, painted diyas.

Dejected, Raghu went back home. "Amma, nobody wants my diyas! I won't go to the market any more."

Amma gave Raghu a hug, and sat beside him. "Do you know why we celebrate Diwali, Raghu?"

"Yes," said Raghu. "It is to celebrate Rama's return to his kingdom, Ayodhya."

"But the Diwali story began many years ago. For fourteen years, Rama lived in the jungle with his wife Sita and brother Laxman. When the wicked king Ravana took Sita away, Rama went to Lanka to fight a battle. Rama had no kingdom and no army. But he did not give up."

"He defeated Ravana and went back to Ayodhya. All the people greeted him with lighted lamps. But Raghu, suppose Rama had given up–we would not celebrate Diwali today. Now tell me, do you want to be like Rama, or do you want to give up?"

Raghu sat and thought about what his mother had said. Then, he took all the money from his piggy bank and went to the market. He bought small pieces of coloured glass, red and yellow paint, silver and gold threads and some glue.

First, Raghu painted the diyas bright. Then, he stuck on the coloured glass, and fixed the silver and gold threads. Now the diyas looked beautiful! How they shone and sparkled in the sun!

He took the diyas to the market. He spread them out, so that everyone could see how beautiful they were. Many came to Raghu, and soon all his diyas were sold. Now Raghu had earned a lot of money!

He wanted to buy crackers, but he knew they made noise, and spread smoke everywhere. So he decided to buy a small doll for his sister, Gita. He would give it to her after Diwali, for Bhai Dooj.

Happy with the morning's work, Raghu picked up the basket and ran all the way home. Hidden inside the basket was one diya.

"See, Amma! I have sold all the diyas. This last one is for you."

"It's beautiful!" said Amma. "We will keep this one for the puja tomorrow."

Diwali day dawned bright and clear. Amma made a rangoli outside the house. She put flowers and sugar toys before the Goddess Laxmi. They all wore new clothes, and ate laddoos, which were soft and sweet.

In the evening, they lighted the diyas in the house and outside in the courtyard. Soon, all the houses were lit up by twinkling diyas.

But the brightest and most beautiful diya was the one that burned before the Goddess Laxmi. It was the one that Raghu had made!

Abdul's Eid

Illustrated by Neeta Gangopadhyay

Abdul's father, Abba, was a tailor. He had been hard at work since morning, stitching buttons on new clothes and ironing them.

Abdul was putting them away in paper bags so that he could later deliver them to Abba's customers. Eid was just two days away. And everyone wore new clothes for Eid!

Abdul's mother, Ammi, was also busy. There was so much to do–washing, cleaning and polishing. She wanted everything to sparkle for Eid.

She had work in the kitchen too–grinding spices, chopping nuts and preparing kebabs.

Every year Muslims, the world over, fast during the holy month of Ramzan. At the end of the month when the new moon shines in the night sky, they celebrate Eid.

The next day, Abdul and his family woke up before sunrise. They ate sweets and drank tea. In the evening, they broke their fast by eating dates, imaratis, rotis and kebabs.

Ammi had brought new clothes for the entire family. There was a kurta-pyjama for Abdul.

Abdul loved his new clothes. Now if only he had a red velvet jacket to go with it!

Abdul had seen the jacket in a shop window. It was made of soft velvet and had a border edged in gold thread. Abdul could imagine himself wearing it on Eid. But when he told Abba about the jacket, Abba shook his head, "Maybe next year, Abdul," he said.

Abdul set out to deliver the new clothes and collect payment from Abba's customers. On the way, he saw Rashid ironing people's clothes.

He waved happily to Gopi, the vegetable seller.

Abdul delivered the new clothes to Saira Chachi. He then went to Naseem Khala's house. She was preparing seviyan for Eid. She smiled at Abdul and gave him some almonds to eat in the evening.

The last stop on his round was Kamla Mausi's house.

She was Ammi's friend. Although Kamla Mausi did not fast during Ramzan, she always came to Abdul's house to celebrate Eid, and would give him eleven rupees as Eidi.

That evening when Abdul was returning home, he again stopped at the shop with the red velvet jacket. But, the jacket was gone! Someone had bought the jacket, Abdul thought sadly.

The next morning it was Eid. And what a wonderful day it was! Abba and Abdul went to the Masjid to offer Namaz. Later all their friends and neighbours came to visit them. "Eid Mubarak!" they said as they greeted each other and shared the seviyan, biryani, kebab and sheer-khurma that Ammi had made.

Abdul greeted everyone and carefully put away the money he received as 'Eidi'. Perhaps he could buy a velvet jacket next year.

Kamla Mausi was the last to visit. She had brought some sweets with her, and told Ammi that her sheer khurma was delicious.

After some time, Kamla Mausi got ready to leave.

Abdul looked towards her wondering if she had forgotten to give him 'Eidi' this year.

Kamala Mausi had reached the door when she turned to Abdul. "No Eidi this time Abdul!" Abdul's face fell.

"But I have something else for you instead!" And from a paper bag she took the red velvet jacket. Abdul could hardly believe his eyes!

He ran to Kamla Mausi and gave her a hug. He quickly wore the jacket and gave her another hug!

That day Abdul was so happy he could hardly stop smiling. He felt the softness of the jacket again and again.

This was the best Eid ever, he thought as he fell asleep, still wearing the red velvet jacket!

Tina's Christmas

Illustrated by Jagdish Joshi

It was Christmas eve and Tina watched the colourful lights on the Christmas tree. There were silver and gold balls, bright ribbons and small gifts hanging from the trees. It looked really beautiful!

But Tina was not happy.

Tina's mother had made a special Christmas cake, with white sugar icing. It stood on the table nearby. There were biscuits, fruits and nuts too. They looked and smelt delicious!

But Tina was not happy.

Next to the table was a large basket. It was full of packets, all tied up in pretty wrapping papers. Tina knew these were Christmas presents, to be opened tomorrow.

But still Tina was not happy.

Just then, the door opened and her mother came in with a small boy. He was Robin, Tina's cousin. Robin's parents were away and he had come to spend Christmas with Tina and her family. And that's why Tina scowled and frowned. She didn't want Robin here for Christmas!

Whenever Robin came he wanted to play with all her toys. Tina didn't like that! Besides, he would fling her doll high up in the air, and wind up her toy car so hard that it almost broke.

He kicked her ball out of the window and threw her books here and there. How Tina wished he had not come here for Christmas or Santa had taken him away!

In the evening the whole family went to the Church. In the centre was the beautiful Nativity scene with small figures of Mary and Joseph and the shepherds. There were toy sheep, lambs and cows in the manger. And in the middle was a crib with the baby Jesus.

The priest told them the story of Christmas. On a cold winter night, all the rooms in the town of Bethlehem were full. So Mary and Joseph took shelter in a manger. A baby boy was born to them. He grew up to be Jesus Christ and spread the message of love and goodwill. Each year, the world celebrates his birthday on Christmas.

After dinner at home, Tina and Robin went upstairs to sleep. In the middle of the night, she suddenly woke up, and sat up in bed. She heard someone crying.

It was Robin. He missed his parents, he said. It was Christmas and he wished he was home.

Poor Robin! Tina went to him. She put her arms around him to comfort him. But he would not stop crying.

Tina brought her new teddy bear and gave it to him. When he did not stop, she gave him her pop-up book and her train set.

Robin stopped crying.

"But you don't like me playing with your toys," he said.

"That's because, I don't like to share my toys. And also because, you spoil them," said Tina.

Robin looked as though he might start crying again.

"But, today is Christmas, so you can play with them too!" smiled Tina.

Next morning, after a special breakfast, they opened all their presents.

Tina saw a book and a badminton set with two racquets and a shuttlecock. Robin got a book and a green car.

Soon, Tina and Robin were out in the garden playing badminton. She found that some games could only be played with others. And sharing her toys was a lot of fun!

Munni's Dussehra

Illustrated by Neeta Gangopadhyay

Munni and her grandpa were going to the Dussehra mela. They waved to her mother and father and got on the bus.

The mela was full of exciting things to see and do. There was a big Ferris wheel and a merry-go-round. There was an elephant taking children for rides. And there were lots and lots of shops.

At one end of the ground were three giant effigies of the demons–Ravana, Kumbhakaran and Meghnad. In the evening, these would be set alight, and there would be fireworks. But there was plenty of time before that. Munni's mother had given her ten rupees, so Nanu and Munni decided to go shopping.

On the way, they passed a group of dancers in bright, colourful clothes. They were dancing with small sticks, as they went round and round. Nanu told Munni that this was the Dandiya Raas, and the dancers had come all the way from Gujarat.

A little further, Munni saw a bright pandal. Outside, a man was blowing a conch shell. Munni and Nanu went in. There was a beautiful statue of the Goddess Durga inside–a lot of women were praying to her. The pandal had been put up by the people of Bengal.

It was time now to visit the shops. What a lot of shops there were–full of clothes, bright toys and colourful balloons. There were glass bangles, ribbons, hair bands and mehendi for the hands. There were also shops selling sweets, ice candy and sherbet. Nearby, a man was making candyfloss.

Munni stopped at one shop after another. She couldn't decide what to buy!

"Have you seen something you like?" asked Nanu.

"I like them all," said Munni. "I want them all!"

Nanu laughed, "You will have to be a magician to buy everything."

Soon, the Ram Leela began and Nanu and Munni sat down to watch. Two men were dressed as Rama and Ravana, while others pretended to fight a battle.

Then the effigies of Ravana, Kumbhakaran and Meghnad were lit. Firecrackers began to burst and the statues of the demons burst into bright red and orange flames.

Finally, with a loud thud, the effigies fell to the ground. Rama won and Ravana lost– the wicked demon was dead. Munni also laughed and clapped her hands.

It was evening now, and time to leave. Nanu and Munni took the bus back home. Suddenly, Munni remembered that she hadn't bought anything with the money she had.

"But I have bought something special for you," Nanu said with a smile.

"Show me, Nanu, please," said Munni.

"Only when we get home!" said Nanu, with a twinkle in his eyes.

As soon as they reached home, Munni asked Nanu to show her the surprise. Nanu opened a bag and took out six books.

They had beautiful pictures of tigers and elephants, flowers and trees, hills and rivers, cars and trains, fields and houses and many little boys and girls!

"You said you wanted everything, didn't you, Munni? See, now you have the whole world in the pages of these books!"

Munni gave Nanu a big hug.

She took the books and kept them near her pillow as she went to sleep.

Tomorrow she would see and read about those wonderful pictures–tomorrow she would go around the world!